Irish Wit
and Wisdom

Daily Words of
Wisdom and Blarney

Martin Hintz

January 1

How sweetly lies old Ireland
Emerald green beyond the foam,
Awakening sweet memories,
Calling the heart back home.

IRISH BLESSING

Martin Hintz is founder and publisher of *The Irish American Post,* one of the nation's most comprehensive news magazines covering Irish and Irish American affairs. From 1981 to 1996, he was the promotions director for Milwaukee Irish Fest, one of the world's largest Irish cultural events. He is the co-author of *Irish Wit and Wisdom* and *Celtic Myths and Legends* and has written and contributed to more than 60 books, in addition to his work on Irish and Celtic topics.

January 4

The Spell-Struck

SHE WALKS as she were moving
Some mystic dance to tread,
So fall her gliding footsteps,
So leans her glistening head.

For once to fairy harping
She danced upon the hill,
And through her brain and bosom
The music pulses still.

Her eyes are bright and tearless,
But wide with yearning pain;
She longs for nothing earthly,
But O! To hear again

The sound that held her listening
Upon her moonlit path!
The rippling fairy music
That filled the lonely rath.

THOMAS W. HAZEN ROLLESTON

Anniversary Gifts

First • Paper
Second • Cotton
Third • Leather
Fourth • Fruit/Flowers
Fifth • Wood
Sixth • Candy/Iron
Seventh • Wool/Copper
Eighth • Bronze/Pottery
Ninth • Pottery/Willow
Tenth • Tin/Aluminum
Eleventh • Steel
Twelfth • Silk/Linen

Thirteenth • Lace
Fourteenth • Ivory
Fifteenth • Crystal
Twentieth • China
Twenty-Fifth • Silver
Thirtieth • Pearls
Thirty-Fifth • Coral
Fortieth • Ruby
Forty-Fifth • Sapphire
Fiftieth • Gold
Fifty-fifth • Emerald
Sixtieth • Diamond

January 5

It's [the love of Irish music] like an addictive drug or ritual, and I couldn't imagine my life without it. Like not having coffee, I get irritated if I can't play.

Dan Beimborn, of the musical group 180 and the Letter G

December

Birthdays & Anniversaries

_____   _____
_____   _____
_____   _____
_____   _____
_____   _____
_____   _____
_____

Birthstone: Turquoise   _____
Flower: Poinsettia   _____

January 6

❖

IT IS, in fact, incredible what a singular passion the Irish gentlemen (though in general excellent-tempered fellows) formerly had for fighting each other and immediately making friends again. A duel was indeed considered a necessary piece of a young man's education, but by no means a ground for future animosity with his opponent.

SIR JONAH BARRINGTON

November

Birthdays & Anniversaries

_____   _____
_____   _____
_____   _____
_____   _____
_____   _____
_____   _____

Birthstone: Topaz
Flower: Chrysanthemum

January 8

O IRELAND! DON'T you hear me shout?
I bid you top o' the mornin'.

JOHN LOCKE

September

Birthdays & Anniversaries

_____   _____
_____   _____
_____   _____
_____   _____
_____   _____
_____   _____
_____   _____

Birthstone: Sapphire
Flower: Aster

January 9

THAT PART of the mind which we call intellect; that part of the mind which deals with thought and argument, reasoning and ideas, is, in the Irish, quick, sharp, strong, active. The Irish mind combines readily and rapidly. It delights in analogies and analysis, in criticism and controversy. Hence, perhaps, the success of the Irish mind at the bar, in the pulpit, in the popular assembly, in all those positions which demand the spontaneous transmission of thinking into speech.

HENRY GILES

August

Birthdays & Anniversaries

_____   _____
_____   _____
_____   _____
_____   _____
_____   _____
_____   _____

Birthstone: Peridot   _____
Flower: Gladiolus   _____

January 10

DANCE LIGHT, for my heart it lies under your feet, love.

JOHN FRANCIS WALLER

July

Birthdays & Anniversaries

_____   _____
_____   _____
_____   _____
_____   _____
_____   _____
_____   _____
_____   _____

Birthstone: Ruby
Flower: Sweet Peas   _____

January 11

NOTHING BUT fun, nothing but wit, nothing but merriment was heard on either side. Here were not only all the bright spirits of the day, but they were met by appointment; they came prepared for the combat, armed for the fight; and certainly never was such a joust of wit and brilliancy. Good stories rained around; jests, repartees, and epigrams flew like lightning; and one had but time to catch some sparkling gem as it glittered, ere another and another succeeded.

CHARLES JAMES LEVER

June

Birthdays & Anniversaries

_____   _____
_____   _____
_____   _____
_____   _____
_____   _____
_____   _____
_____

Birthstone: Pearl
Flower: Rose   _____

January 12

WESTWARD THE course of empire takes its way,
The four first acts already past;
A fifth shall close the drama with the day—
Time's noblest offspring is the last.

BISHOP GEORGE BERKELEY

May

Birthdays & Anniversaries

_____   _____

_____   _____

_____   _____

_____   _____

_____   _____

_____   _____

Birthstone: Emerald

Flower: Lily of the Valley

January 13

My Dark Rosaleen

THE VERY soul within my
   breast
Is wasted for you, love!
The heart in my bosom faints
To think of you, my Queen,
My life of life, my saint of
   saints,

My dark Rosaleen!
My own Rosaleen!
To hear your sweet and sad
   complaints,
My dark Rosaleen!

JAMES CLARENCE MANGAN

April

Birthdays & Anniversaries

_____   _____

_____   _____

_____   _____

_____   _____

_____   _____

_____   _____

Birthstone: Diamond

Flower: Daisy or Lily   _____

January 14

ALL MY life long I have delighted in rivers, rivulets, rills, fierce torrents, tearing their rocky beds, gliding, dimpled brooks kissing a daisied marge. The tinkle, or murmur, or deep-resounding roll, or raving roar of running water is of all sounds my ears hear even now the most homely.

JOHN MITCHEL

March

Birthdays & Anniversaries

_____   _____

_____   _____

_____   _____

_____   _____

_____   _____

_____   _____

Birthstone: Aquamarine   _____
Flower: Violet   _____

January 15

A VERY STRIKING characteristic of an Irishman is his unwillingness to be outdone.

SAMUEL LOVER

February

Birthdays & Anniversaries

_____   _____

_____   _____

_____   _____

_____   _____

_____   _____

_____   _____

_____   _____

Birthstone: Amethyst
Flower: Primrose   _____

January 16

TWINKLE, TWINKLE, little star,
Now we find out what you are,
When unto the midnight sky
We the spectroscope apply.

SIR ROBERT STAWELL BALL

January

Birthdays & Anniversaries

_____   _____

_____   _____

_____   _____

_____   _____

_____   _____

_____   _____

Birthstone: Garnet   _____

Flower: Carnation   _____

January 17

THE OLDER the fiddle
the sweeter the tune.

IRISH PROVERB

December 31

I'VE MADE a resolution not to destroy my ego or self-esteem by declaring any New Year's resolutions. I usually break them within a week, so I decided to give up on them.

FRANK SHERIDAN, IRISH CONSUL

January 18

How happy is the sailor's life,
From coast to coast to roam;
In every port he finds a wife,
In every land a home.
He loves to range, he's nowhere strange;
He ne'er will turn his back
To friend or foe; no masters, no;
My life for honest Jack.

ISAAC BICKERSTAFF

December 30

YOU MATCHLESS nine, to my aid incline,
Assist my genius while I declare
My lovesick pain for a beauteous dame,
Whose killing charms did me ensnare;
Sly little Cupid has knocked me stupid;
In grief I mourn upon my oath;
My frame's declining, I'm so repining
For Hannah Healy, the pride of Howth.

IRISH STREET BALLAD

January 19

No Fish Here

HOPING TO land a few fish? Don't bother dipping your line into the River Boyle, in western Ireland. According to legend, St. Patrick once fell into the river and cursed it on the spot. The fishing has been poor ever since.

December 29

Wᴴᴇɴ ꜰɪʀꜱᴛ to this country a stranger I came,
I placed my affections on a comely fair maid,
She was proper, tall and handsome, in every degree,
She's the flower of this country and the Rose of Ardee.

I courted lovely Mary at the age of sixteen,
Her waist it was slender, and her carriage genteel;
Till at length a young weaver came for her to see,
Stole the flower of this country and the Rose of Ardee.

Iʀɪꜱʜ ꜱᴛʀᴇᴇᴛ ʙᴀʟʟᴀᴅ

January 20

Sweet is a voice in the land of gold,
Sweet is the calling of wild birds bold;
Sweet is the shriek of the heron hoar,
Sweet fall the billows of Bundatrore.
Sweet is the sound of the blowing breeze,
Sweet is the blackbird's song in the trees;
Lovely the sheen of the shining sun,
Sweet is the thrush over Casacon.

GEORGE SIGERSON

December 28

ONE OF the best things about working with your family is that you can't get fired.

CAITLIN LEAHY, MUSICIAN IN HER FATHER'S BAND, LEAHY'S LUCK

January 21

HE WAS a great hand at settling and arranging duels, being what we generally call in Ireland a *judgmatical* sort of a man—a word which, I think, might be introduced with advantage into the English vocabulary.

WILLIAM MAGINN

December 27

ALL DAY in exquisite air
The song clomb an invisible stair,
Flight on flight, story on story,
Into the dazzling glory.

KATHARINE TYNAN-HINKSON

January 22

DENNIS WAS hearty when Dennis was young,
High was his step in the jig that he sprung,
He had the looks an' the sootherin tongue,—
An' he wanted a girl wid a fortune.
Nannie was gray-eyed an' Nannie was tall,
Fair was the face hid in-undher her shawl,
Troth! an' he liked her the best o' them all,—
But she'd not a *traneen* to her fortune.

MOIRA O'NEILL

December 26

A MAN WITHOUT learning, and wearing fine clothes,
Is like a pig with a gold ring in his nose.

GERALD GRIFFIN

January 23

IRELAND—THAT most
ancient and holy
island in the
western sea...

THOMAS N. BURKE

December 25

THOSE EVENING bells! those evening bells!
How many a tale their music tells,
Of youth, and home, and that sweet time,
When last I heard their soothing chime.

THOMAS MOORE

January 24

EACH POET with a different talent writes,
One praises, one instructs, another bites.

WENTWORTH DILLON, EARL OF ROSCOMMON

December 24

ROLL FORTH, my
song, like the
rushing river.

JAMES CLARENCE MANGAN

January 25

IN THE Valley of Shanganagh, where the songs of skylarks teem,
And the rose perfumes the ocean-breeze, as love the hero's dream,
'Twas there I wooed my Maggie. In her dark eyes there did dwell
A secret that the billows knew, but yet could never tell.
Oh! light as fairy tread her voice fell on my bounding heart;
And like the wild bee to the flower still clinging we would part.

JOHN MARTLEY

December 23

O PEGGY BRADY, you are my darlin',
You are my lookin'-glass from night to mornin',
I'd rather have you without a farthin'
Than Susy Gallagher, wid her house and garden.

IRISH STREET BALLAD

January 26

IN A TIME like ours, changes of every kind move faster than they did in the days of darkness and isolation; and, though there are moments when clouds seem to settle down over Ireland or over Europe as a whole, yet if we compare the condition of the world now with that of a century ago, we find ample grounds for a faith in the increasing strength of the forces which make for righteousness and peace.

JAMES BRYCE

December 22

THERE WAS once a poor
widow woman who had
a daughter that was as
handsome as the day,
and as lazy as a pig,
saving your presence.

PATRICK KENNEDY

January 27

The Buried Forests of Erin

THERE WERE trees in Tir-Conal of the territories
In Erin's ancient yet remembered days,
Where now to clothe the leagues of bogland lonely
Is only heather brown or gorse ablaze:
Where rivers go from source to sea unshaded,
Where shine in desolate moors the scattered lakes,
And sedges only, where once were willows,
And curlews where were deer in woodland brakes.

ALICE MILLIGAN

December 21

OH, THE mountain gates of dreamland have
   opened once again,
And the sound of song and dancing falls upon the
   ears of men;
And the Land of Youth lies gleaming flushed with
   opal light and mirth,
And the old enchantment lingers in the honey
   heart of earth.

GEORGE W. RUSSELL

January 28

EITHER MARRY very
young, or become a
monk very young.

IRISH PROVERB

December 20

FINALLY, ENCIRCLING all, is the perpetual presence of the sea, with its foaming, thunderous life or its days of dreamy peace; round the silver sands or furrowed cliffs that gird the island our white waves rush forever, murmuring the music of eternity.

Such the land of Eire, very old, yet full of perpetual youth; a thousand times darkened by sorrow, yet with a heart of living gladness; too often visited by evil and pale death, yet welling ever up in unconquerable life . . .

CHARLES JOHNSTON

January 29

The Groves of Blarney

THE GROVES of Blarney
They look so charming,
Down by the purling
Of sweet silent streams,
Being banked with posies,
That spontaneous grow there,
Planted in order
By the sweet rock close.

RICHARD ALFRED MILLIKIN

December 19

MISS MASSY has a hen,
She lays guggies now and then:
Sometimes two and sometimes ten,—
And out with you, my little spotted hen!

RICHARD O'KENNEDY

January 30

So we sat around the fire again, while without the storm howled, and the fierce gusts which swept the valley seemed at times as if they would break the door, lift off the roof, or in some way annihilate the time-worn cabin which gave us shelter.

BRAM STOKER

December 18

DO ENGINE drivers, I wonder, eternally wish they were small boys?

BRIAN O'NOLAN, *THE BEST OF MYLES*

January 31

MOLLY MULDOON was an Irish girl,
And as fine a one
As you'd look upon
In the cot of a peasant or hall of an earl.
Her teeth were white, though not of pearl,
And dark was her hair, though it did not curl;
Yet few who gazed on her teeth and her hair,
But owned that a power o' beauty was there.

19TH CENTURY IRISH STREET BALLAD

December 17

WHAT IS a gentleman? Is it a thing
Decked with a scarf-pin, a chain, and a ring,
Dressed in a suit of immaculate style,
Sporting an eye-glass, a lisp, and a smile;
Talking of operas, concerts, and balls,
Evening assemblies, and afternoon calls;
Sunning himself at "homes" and bazaars,
Whistling mazurkas and smoking cigars?

MRS. POWER O'DONOGHUE

February 1

The Pillar Towers of Ireland

THE PILLAR towers of Ireland, how wondrously they stand
By the lakes and rushing rivers, through the valleys of our
land!
In mystic file, through the isle, they lift their heads sublime,
These gray old pillar temples—these conquerors of time!

DENIS FLORENCE MCCARTHY

December 16

SHE HAD always been the belle of the village. At patterns and fairs, at wakes and dances, Mave was the admiration of all. She was tall and strong for her eighteen years, with a neat, well-shaped head crowned with a coronet of nut-brown hair; a skin like the inside of a shell, so dainty its coloring; and eyes of the deepest blue, that looked black in the shadow of the long dark lashes.

LADY GILBERT

February 2

I HAVE KNOWN some men possessed of good qualities which were very serviceable to others, but useless to themselves; like a sun-dial on the front of a house, to inform the neighbors and passengers, but not the owner within.

JONATHAN SWIFT

December 15

AFTER READING the diaries of my great-grandfathers, I discovered the real voices of my ancestors. I drew them out. They had to be bribed.

TOM RUSSELL, SONGWRITER

February 3

SHE'S AS headstrong
as an allegory on
the banks of Nile!

RICHARD BRINSLEY SHERIDAN

December 14

THE STARS are watching, the winds are playing;
They see me kneeling, they see me praying;
They hear me still, through the long night saying
*Asthore mahcree,** I love you, I love you!

MRS. KEVIN IZOD O'DOHERTY
***TREASURE OF MY HEART**

February 4

The Last Desire

WHEN THE time comes for me to die,
To-morrow, or some other day,
If God should bid me make reply,
"What wilt thou?" I shall say:
"O God, thy world was great and fair!
Have thanks for all my days have seen;
Yet grant me peace from things that were
And things that might have been."

THOMAS W. HAZEN ROLLESTON

December 13

THERE IS not in the wide world a valley so sweet
As that vale in whose bosom the bright waters meet;
O, the last rays of feeling and life must depart,
Ere the bloom of that valley shall fade from my heart.

Sweet vale of Avoca! how calm could I rest
In thy bosom of shade, with the friends I love best,
Where the storms that we feel in this cold world should cease,
And our hearts, like thy waters, be mingled in peace.

THOMAS MOORE

February 5

Kitty of Coleraine

AS BEAUTIFUL Kitty one morning was tripping
With a pitcher of milk for the fair of Coleraine,
When she saw me she stumbled, the pitcher down tumbled,
And all the sweet buttermilk watered the plain.
"Oh, what shall I do now? 'Twas looking at you now!
I'm sure such a pitcher I'll ne'er see again.
'Twas the pride of my dairy. Oh, Barney McCleary,
You're sent as a plague to the girls of Coleraine."

CHARLES DAWSON SHANLY

December 12

THOUGH THERE is no bone in the tongue, it has frequently broken a man's head.

IRISH PROVERB

February 6

FIRELIGHT WILL not let you read fine stories, but it's warm and you won't see the dust on the floor.

IRISH PROVERB

December 11

Down by the Salley Gardens

Down by the salley gardens my love and I did meet;
She passed the salley gardens with little snow-white feet.
She bid me take love easy, as the leaves grow on the tree;
But I, being young and foolish, with her could not agree.

In a field by the river my love and I did stand,
And on my leaning shoulder she laid a snow-white hand.
She bid me take life easy, as the grass grows on the weirs;
But I was young and foolish, and now am full of tears.

WILLIAM BUTLER YEATS

February 7

MAY YOU have the hindsight
to know where you've been
and foresight to know where you're going
and the insight to know when you're going too far.

IRISH TOAST

December 10

Office Politics

OVERHEARD IN the White House pub and restaurant in Kinsale, as one businessman was talking to another, "Whenever I want to kill time, I call a committee meeting. It's the ideal weapon."

February 8

We're always looking for new blood.

Declan McIntyre, director of the Bram Stoker International Seminar School

December 9

IF YOU would like to see the height of hospitality,
The cream of kindly welcome,
   and the core of cordiality:
Joys of all the olden time—you're wishing
   to recall again?
Come down to Donovans,
   and there you'll meet them all again.

FRANCIS A. FAHY

February 9

THE GAEL is not like other men; the spade, and the lom, and the sword are not for him. But a destiny more glorious than that of Rome, more glorious than that of Britain, awaits him: to become the savior of idealism in modern intellectual and social life.

PATRICK PEARSE, IRISH NOVELIST

December 8

"**S**IR," SHOUTED Johnson, "if you were not a clergyman I would say that you were a very impertinent fellow!"

FRANK FRANKFORT MOORE

February 10

COME TO me, dearest, I'm lonely without thee;
Day-time and night-time I'm thinking about thee;
Night-time and day-time in dreams I behold thee,
Unwelcome the waking that ceases to fold thee.
Come to me, darling, my sorrows to lighten,
Come in thy beauty to bless and to brighten,
Come in thy womanhood, meekly and lowly,
Come in thy lovingness, queenly and holy.

JOSEPH BRENAN

December 7

THREE HERMITS sought peace and quietude in a valley far remote from the haunts of men. At the end of a year one remarked, "It's a fine life we are having here." After another year the second hermit replied, "It is." When a third year had elapsed, the remaining hermit broke into the conversation with the threat, "If I cannot get peace here, I'll go back to the world!"

MICHAEL MACDONAGH

February 11

Now Felix Magee puts his pipes to his knee,
And with flourish so free sets each couple in motion;
With a cheer and a bound the boys patter the ground,
The maids move around just like swans on the ocean,
Cheeks bright as the rose, feet light as the doe's,
Now coyly retiring, now boldly advancing;
Search the world all around, from the sky to the ground,
No such sight can be found as an Irish lass dancing.

John Francis Waller

December 6

MY MISTRESS so fair is, no language or art
Can describe her perfection in every part;
Her mien's so genteel,
With such ease she can kill,
Each look with new passion she captures my heart.

THOMAS DUFFET

February 12

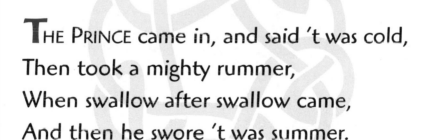

THE PRINCE came in, and said 't was cold,
Then took a mighty rummer,
When swallow after swallow came,
And then he swore 't was summer.

RICHARD BRINSLEY SHERIDAN

December 5

MANY PEOPLE say my movies were ahead of their times because I always met the man toe-to-toe. But since the early days, Irish women have always been strong and always worked hard.

MAUREEN O'HARA, ACTRESS

February 13

WHEN A true genius appears in the world you may know him by this sign, that the dunces are all in confederacy against him.

JONATHAN SWIFT

December 4

GOD BLESS the gray mountains of dark Donegal,
God bless Royal Aileach, the pride of them all;
For she sits evermore like a queen on her throne,
And smiles on the valley of Green Innishowen.
And fair are the valleys of Green Innishowen,
And hardy the fishers that call them their own—
A race that nor traitor nor coward have known
Enjoy the fair valleys of Green Innishowen.

SIR CHARLES GAVAN DUFFY

February 14

MY HEART in the heat of devotion so
  beats to you,
'T is just like a little child crying for
  sweets to you!

MICHAEL HOGAN

December 3

EVERY TERRIER is
bold in his own
doorway.

IRISH PROVERB

February 15

MY NAME is Patrick Sheehan,
My years are thirty-four;
Tipperary is my native place,
Not far from Galtymore:
I came of honest parents,
But now they're lying low;
And many a pleasant day I spent
In the Glen of Aherlow.

CHARLES JOSEPH KICKHAM

December 2

O, DID YOU not hear of Kate Kearney?
She lives on the banks of Killarney,
From the glance of her eye shun danger and fly,
For fatal's the glance of Kate Kearney!
For that eye is so modestly beaming,
You'd ne'er think of mischief she's dreaming,
Yet oh, I can tell how fatal's the spell
That lurks in the eye of Kate Kearney.

LADY MORGAN

February 16

THOU SAYEST that fate is frosty nothing,
But love the flame of souls that are:
"Two spirits approach, and at their touching,
Behold! an everlasting star."

WILLIAM LARMINIE

December 1

THE GLOOMY way is brightened when we walk with those we love.

J. O'DONOVAN ROSSA

February 17

IF YOU searched the county o' Carlow, ay, and back again,
Wicklow too, and Wexford, for that matter you might try,
Never the equal of Old Pedhar would you crack again'—
Never such another would delight your Irish eye!
Mirth, mime and mystery, all were close combined in him,
Divelment and drollery right to the very core,
As many tricks and turns as a two-year-old you'd find in him—
In Old Pedhar Carthy from Clonmore!
Old Pedhar, Old Pedhar, Old Pedhar Carthy!
Old Pedhar Carthy from Clonmore!

PATRICK J. McCALL

November 30

AT THE mid hour of night, when stars are weeping, I fly
To the lone vale we loved, when life shone warm in thine eye;
And I think oft, if spirits can steal from the regions of air,
To revisit past scenes of delight, thou wilt come to me there,
And tell me our love is remembered, even in the sky.

THOMAS MOORE

February 18

WHAT WE really need are poems to polka to.

R. M. RYAN, POET

November 29

Kate of Garnavilla

HAVE YOU been at Garnavilla?
Have you seen at Garnavilla
Beauty's train trip o'er the plain
With lovely Kate of Garnavilla?
Oh! she's pure as virgin snows
Ere they light on woodland hill-O;
Sweet as dew-drop on wild rose
Is lovely Kate of Garnavilla!

EDWARD LYSAGHT

February 19

DANCING—inspiring—
My wild blood firin';
Oh! terrible glory—
Oh! beautiful siren—
Come, tell the old story—
Come, light up my fancy, and open my heart.

JOSEPH SHERIDAN LE FANU

November 28

IRISH ORATORY is, as a rule, pitched in a high key, and the conversational manner is seldom employed. But no speeches which have borne the test of time are conversational, nor can polished chat ever rise to the dignity of eloquence.

JOHN F. TAYLOR

February 20

T*H' ANÁM an Dhia.* * But there it is—
The dawn on the hills of Ireland!
God's angels lifting back the night's black veil
From the fair, sweet face of my sireland!
O Ireland isn't it grand you look—
Like a bride in her rich adornin'?
And with all the pent-up love of my heart
I bid you the top o' the mornin'!

JOHN LOCKE
*MY SOUL TO GOD

November 27

ONE MAY live without one's friends, but not without one's pipe.

IRISH PROVERB

February 21

OH, THE FERN, the fern, the Irish hill fern,
That girds our blue lakes from Lough Ine to Lough Erne,
That waves on our crags like the plume of a king,
And bends like a nun over clear well and spring.
The fairies' tall palm-tree, the heath-bird's fresh nest,
And the couch the red-deer deems the sweetest and best;
With the free winds to fan it, and dew-drops to gem,
Oh, what can ye match with its beautiful stem?

ARTHUR GERALD GEOGHEGAN

November 26

Sense of Old

THEY (the Gaelic people) have had an almost exaggerated sense of the importance of the past. The poet to them was not so much a maker as a recorder: not a deviser of stories, but one who could put new life through skilful words into actions that passed long ago. Literature maintained the national life...

STEPHEN GWYNN

February 22

THERE IS in the Irish mind an idealism which, more or less, influences all its faculties, and which naturally disposes the Irish to what is intensive and poetic. Many of the faults and failings in Irish character may perhaps be traced to this peculiarity.

HENRY GILES

November 25

O'DRISCOLL DROVE with a
song
The wild duck and the drake
From the tall and tufted
reeds
Of the drear Hart Lake.

And he saw how the reeds
grew dark
At the coming of night tide,

And dreamed of the long
dim hair
Of Bridget his bride.

He heard, while he sang and
dreamed,
A piper piping away,
And never was piping so sad,
And never was piping so gay.

WILLIAM BUTLER YEATS

February 23

I'LL LOVE thee evermore,
Eileen Aroon!
I'll bless thee o'er and o'er,
Eileen Aroon!
Oh, for thy sake I'll tread
Where the plains of Mayo
    spread,
By hope still fondly led,
Eileen Aroon!

Oh, how may I gain thee,
Eileen Aroon?
Shall feasting entertain thee,
Eileen Aroon?
I would range the world
    wide,
With love alone to guide,
To win thee for my bride,
Eileen Aroon!

THOMAS FURLONG

November 24

MY DAD died on cue.

BILLY ROCHE, IRISH PLAYWRIGHT

February 24

LIFE IS not life
without thee.
THOMAS FURLONG

November 23

WHERE THE sea flows over the full fresh water
My love I saw under still boughs;
And swimming my boat on that tidal river,
I took my moorings by her greenhouse.

There were many ladies along the Claddagh
Taking air by each garden tree—
All taking air in that early evening,
And none so quiet as my lady.

F. R. HIGGINS

February 25

IN A LITTLE city like Dublin one meets every person whom one knows within a few days. Around each bend in the road there is a friend, an enemy, a bore striding towards you.

JAMES STEPHENS,
THE CHARWOMAN'S DAUGHTER

November 22

Howling Good Time

THE IRISH *bean sidhe,* the Celtic death goddess, is pronounced "banshee" in English. Her wails, which foretell death, are called the *caoin* in Irish and "keen" in English. The word means lament.

The *bean sidhe* rides about the countryside in a huge coach pulled by four headless horses. If the *bean sidhe* knocks on the door, don't open it. You'll get a bowlful of blood in your face if you do.

February 26

You and I

I KNOW WHAT will happen, sweet,
When you and I are one;
Calm and bright and very fleet,
All our days will run.
Fond and kind our words will be,
Mixed no more with sighs;
Thoughts too fine for words we'll see
Within each others eyes.

TIMOTHY DANIEL SULLIVAN

November 21

CÉAD MÍLE fáilte* they'll give you down at
  Donovans,
As cheery as the springtime and Irish as the
  cannawaun * *
The wish of my heart is, if ever I had any one—
That every luck that lightens life may light upon the
  Donovans.

FRANCIS A. FAHY
* A HUNDRED THOUSAND WELCOMES
* * BOG-COTTON

February 27

MAY YOU have warm words on a cold evening,
a full moon on a dark night,
and a smooth road all the way to your door.

IRISH TOAST

November 20

INTO MY heart unsought she came,
A wasting flame, a haunting care;
Into my heart of hearts, ah, why?
And left a sigh for ever there.

ALFRED PERCEVAL GRAVES

February 28

To DRINK a toast,
A proctor roast,
Or bailiff as the case is,
To kiss your wife,
Or take your life
At ten or fifteen paces;
To keep game cocks—to hunt the fox,
To drink in punch the Solway
With debts galore, but fun far more;
Oh, that's the man for Galway.

CHARLES JAMES LEVER

November 19

EVERY DAY I fed the flocks, and prayed frequently during the day; my love of God increased more and more, and my fear and faith in him were augmented, so that in one day I prayed almost a hundred times, and as often in the night: while I tarried on the mountains and in the woods, I was roused to pray both in the snow, frost, and rain; neither did I feel any pain from it nor lassitude, as I think, because my soul was then ardent.

CONFESSION OF ST. PATRICK

February 29

I HAVE ALWAYS been a strong, opinionated, tough woman.

MAUREEN O'HARA

November 18

O Were You on the Mountain?

O WERE YOU on the mountain, and saw you my Love?
And saw you my own one, my queen and my dove?
And saw you the maiden with the step firm and free?
O say, was she pining in sorrow like me?

I was up on the mountain and saw there your Love,
I saw there your own one, your queen and your dove;
I saw there the maiden with the step firm and free,
And she was not pining in sorrow like thee.

DOUGLAS HYDE

March 1

BRAVE OLD Ireland is the land of Fairies, but of all the various descriptions there isn't one to be compared with the Leprechaun, in the regard of cunning and 'cuteness. Now if you don't know what a Leprechaun is, I'll tell you. Why, then—save us and keep us from harm, for they are queer chaps to *gosther* about—a Leprechaun is the fairies' shoemaker: and a mighty conceited little fellow he is, I assure you, and very mischievous . . .

JOHN BROUGHAM

November 17

ONLY WHEN you sit
down to write, do
you discover what you
want to say. You
never know when you
are going to arrive.

PAUL MULDOON, POET

March 2

The Bells of Shandon

I'VE HEARD bells chiming
Full many a clime in,
Tolling sublime in
Cathedral shrine;
While at a glib rate
Brass tongues would vibrate,
But all their music
Spoke naught like thine;
For memory, dwelling
On each proud swelling
Of the belfry, knelling
Its bold notes free,
Made the bells of Shandon
Sound far more grand on
The pleasant waters
Of the River Lee.

FRANCIS SYLVESTER MAHONY

November 16

THIS NATION pays a laudable and industrious regard to their musical pursuits, and excel, in this particular, every other people. Their movements in music are quick and sweet, their melody and concord are in complete harmony.

JOHN MITCHEL

March 3

WHERE THE tongue slips, it speaks the truth.

IRISH PROVERB

November 15

The Irish Language

THE LANGUAGE of Erin is brilliant as gold;
It shines with a lustre unrivalled of old.
Even glanced at by strangers by whom 'tis unknown
It dazzles their eyes with a light all its own!

JAMES CLARENCE MANGAN

March 4

I FOUND IN Munster, unfettered of any,
Kings and queens and poets a many,
Poets well-skilled in music and measure,
Prosperous doings, mirth and pleasure.

**ALDFRID, KING OF NORTHUMBRIA, "ALDFRID'S ITINERARY"
(7TH CENTURY; AFTER A VISIT TO IRELAND)**

November 14

Connla's Well

I THINK, WHEN night towers up aloft and shakes the
   trembling dew,
How every high and lonely thought that thrills
   my spirit through
Is but a shining berry dropped down through the purple air,
And from the magic tree of life the fruit falls everywhere.

GEORGE W. RUSSELL

March 5

WE SHALL not attempt to offer any advice to the female sex on a question as to the best manner of seeking admiration. It would be a decided impertinence for us to endeavor to lecture women about a science wherein they are confessedly our superiors.

EDWARD MARTYN

November 13

OFTEN ON quiet
afternoons, I would
climb the steps into the
church, make an
offering and think
quietly to myself of
who I was and where I
had come from.

EAMONN WALL, POET

March 6

Kathleen O'More

HER HAIR glossy black, her eyes were dark blue,
Her color still changing, her smiles ever new—
So pretty was Kathleen, my sweet little Kathleen
My Kathleen O'More!

GEORGE NUGENT REYNOLDS

November 12

Beauty

FAR UP the dim twilight fluttered
Moth wings of vapour and flame,
The lights danced over the mountains,
Star after star they came.

The lights grew thicker unheeded,
But silent and still were we,
Our hearts were drunk with a beauty
Our eyes could never see.

GEORGE RUSSELL

March 7

MAY THE face of every good news
And the back of every bad news
Be towards us.

IRISH BLESSING

November 11

The Outlaw of Loch Lene

Oh, MANY a day have I made good ale in the glen,
That came not of stream or malt,
   like the brewing of men.
My bed was the ground,
   my roof the greenwood above,
And the wealth that I sought,
   one fair kind glance from my love.

JEREMIAH CALLANAN

March 8

ON THE eighth (of the month) Brigit was born, on a Thursday especially: on the eighteenth she took the veil: in the eighty-eighth (year of her age) she went to heaven. With eight virgins was Brigit consecrated, according to the number of the eight beatitudes of the Gospel which she fulfilled, and of them it was the beatitude of mercy that Brigit chose.

WHITLEY STOKES

November 10

MAY THE hinges
of our friendship
never grow rusty.

OLD IRISH TOAST

March 9

LOVE THAT my Life began,
Love, that will close life's span,
Love that grows ever by love-giving:
Love, from the first to last,
Love, till all life be passed,
Love that loves on after living!

GEORGE SIGERSON

November 9

Winter Evening

BUT THE rain is gone by, and the day's dying out in a
   splendor;
There is flight as of many gold wings in the heart of the sky:
God's birds, it may be, who return from their ministry tender,
Flying home from the earth, like the earth-birds when
   darkness is nigh.

KATHARINE TYNAN-HINKSON

March 10

GODSPEED IF you know the way;
if you don't, why not stay home.

**BETSA MARSH, DREAMING UP A NEW MOTTO
FOR THE IRISH HIGHWAY DEPARTMENT**

November 8

OF PRIESTS we can offer a charmin' variety,
Far renowned for larnin' and piety;
Still, I'd advance ye widout impropriety,
Father O'Flynn as the flower of them all.
CHORUS:
Here's a health to you, Father O'Flynn,
Sláinte, and *sláinte,* and *sláinte* agin;
Powerfulest preacher, and
Tinderest teacher, and
Kindliest creature in ould Donegal.

ALFRED PERCEVAL GRAVES

March 11

FADING RAPIDLY are the days when the spoken word satisfied a yearning for insights into whatever there was to know about the world, where words carefully chosen and artfully expressed carried us beyond the mundane demands of getting through another day.

TOM WALSH

November 7

THE SILENT bird is hid in the boughs,
The scythe is hid in the corn,
The lazy oxen wink and drowse,
The grateful sheep are shorn;
Redder and redder burns the rose,
The lily was ne'er so pale,
Stiller and stiller the river flows
Along the path to the vale.

LADY GILBERT

March 12

Dry Be That Tear

ASK'ST THOU how long my love shall stay,
When all that's new is past?
How long? Ah! Delia, can I say,
How long my life shall last?
Dry be that tear, be hushed that sigh;
At least I'll love thee till I die—
Hushed be that sigh.

RICHARD BRINSLEY SHERIDAN

November 6

ART IS the most intense mode of individualism that the world has known.

OSCAR WILDE, *THE SOUL OF MAN UNDER SOCIALISM*

March 13

THIS LAND is a region of dreams and trifles.

GEORGE BERKELEY, *THE QUERIST*

November 5

The Leprechaun

He HAMMERED and sang with tiny voice,
And sipped his mountain dew;
Oh! I laughed to think he was caught at last,
But the fairy was laughing, too.

ROBERT DWYER JOYCE

March 14

The Maid of Cloghroe

As I ROVED out, at Faha, one morning,
Where Adrum's tall groves were in view—
When Sol's lucid beams were adorning,
And the meadows were spangled with dew—
Reflecting, in deep contemplation,
On the state of my country kept low,
I perceived a fair juvenile female
On the side of the hill of Cloghroe.

19TH CENTURY IRISH STREET BALLAD

November 4

WHO DREAMED
that beauty passes
like a dream?

WILLIAM BUTLER YEATS

March 15

O, THE DAYS of the Kerry dancing,
O, the ring of the piper's tune!

JAMES LYMAN MOLLOY

November 3

WHERE'ER I roam, whatever realms to see,
My heart untraveled fondly turns to thee...

OLIVER GOLDSMITH

March 16

THE WINTER fleeteth like a dream.
The rain is past and o'er;
The sea is lit with sunny gleam,
The hills are white no more.

GEORGE ARTHUR GREENE

November 2

Iт's EASIER to improve talent in an enthusiastic musician than to create enthusiasm in a talented musician.

PHIL COULTER, MUSICIAN

March 17

THE MAN known as St. Patrick is an historically controversial figure. According to whom you believe, he was one person, three people or didn't exist at all. Whatever the truth, he is the patron saint of Ireland.

MORGAN LLYWELYN

November 1

AN AGED lady, getting into a cab in Dublin, said to the driver, "Help me in, my good man, for I'm very old." "Begor, ma'am," said he, "no matter what age you are, you don't look it."

MICHAEL MACDONAGH

March 18

The Green Little Shamrock

THERE'S A dear little plant that grows in our isle,
'Twas St. Patrick himself sure that set it.
It thrives through the bog, through the brake,
   and the mireland;
And he called it the dear little shamrock of Ireland.

ANDREW CHERRY

October 31

WHEN DEATH comes, it is not enough to have been charitable; and it is not right to touch the body or lay it out for a couple of hours; for the soul should be given time to fight for itself, and to go up to judgment. And sometimes it is not willing to go.

LADY AUGUSTA GREGORY

March 19

THE EARTH, together with all it *spontaneously* produces, is the free and common property of all mankind, of natural right, and by the grant of God:—and all men being equal, no man, therefore, has a right to appropriate exclusively to himself any part or portion thereof, except with and by the *common consent* and *agreement* of all other men.

JAMES FINTAN LALOR

October 30

CERTAINLY, IF you take from art its martyrdom, you will take from it its glory.

WILLIAM BUTLER YEATS

March 20

ON THE plains of
Tipperary the stranger
is like a king.

MRS. KEVIN IZOD O'DOHERTY

October 29

Ireland Origin

EIRE WAS the name of a beautiful queen who welcomed conquering warriors to the island. Many years later, when the Vikings were invading the land, their pronunciation of the soft sound came out as "Ira." So the people of Eire became Ira-ish and the island was known as Ira-land.

March 21

Oh, LITTLE lonely mountain spot!
Your place within my heart will be
Apart from all Life's busy lot
A true, sweet, solemn memory.

Rose Kavanagh

October 28

'**T**WAS THEN my bold peeler
Made after the squealer;
He fetched him a lick
Of a murdering stick;
His shriek spread from Ireland,
My own beloved sireland;
And raised a commotion
Beyond the wide ocean.

FRANCIS A. FAHY

March 22

ALL YE who love the springtime—
 and who but loves it well
When the little birds do sing, and
 the buds begin to swell!—
Think not ye ken its beauty, or know
 its face so dear,
Till ye look upon old Ireland in the
 dawning o' the year!

MARY ELIZABETH BLAKE

October 27

THE WHOLE nation of the Irish are strong in their persons, peculiarly active, possessing a brave and elevated mind; sharp in their intellects and warlike. Life is not regarded in their propensities; labor, cold, and hunger are overlooked; their passions are strong in love; they are hospitable to strangers, sincere in their attachments, and in their quarrels implacable: too credulous, greedy of glory, they will resist insult and injustice, and most ardent in all their acts.

JOHN MITCHEL

March 23

A CAREFUL STUDY of the Irish novelists is necessary to understand the history of Ireland for the last hundred and fifty years, and the material is plentiful and easy of access.

MAURICE FRANCIS EGAN

October 26

SLEEP, BABY dear,
Sleep without fear,
Mother's two arms are clasped
around you.

ALFRED PERCEVAL GRAVES

March 24

I SEE IN Ireland a miraculous and divine history, a life and destiny invisible, lying hid within her visible life.

CHARLES JOHNSTONE

October 25

THE OX is lowing, the winter is creeping in, the summer is gone.

LADY AUGUSTA GREGORY

March 26

THE ANCIENT Irish druids do not appear to have been priests in any sense of the word. They were...men of knowledge and power—"men of science," as they were often designated; they knew the arts of healing and divination, and they were skilled above all in magic. In fact, the Irish druids were magicians, neither more nor less; and hence the Gaelic word for "druidical" is almost always applied where we should use the word "magical."

PATRICK WESTON JOYCE

October 23

FALL IN love if
you can. It is
easy—nothing
easier to a poet.

FRANCIS A. FAHY

March 27

To be happy's to be wise.

GEORGE OGLE

October 22

Oh, Phaudrig Crohoore was the broth of a boy,
And he stood six foot eight;
And his arm was as round as another man's thigh—
'T is Phaudrig was great.
And his hair was as black as the shadows of night—
And hung over the scars left from many a fight;
And his voice, like the thunder, was deep, strong, and loud
And his eye like the lightning from under the cloud.

Joseph Sheridan Le Fanu

March 28

I AM A friar of orders gray:
As down the valley
   I take my way,
I pull not blackberry,
   haw, or hip,
Good store of venison
   does fill my scrip:
My long bead-roll
   I merrily chaunt,
Where'er I walk,

no money I want;
And why I'm so plump the
   reason I'll tell—
Who leads a good life is sure
   to live well.
What baron or squire
Or knight of the shire
Lives half so well
   as a holy friar!

JOHN O'KEEFE

October 21

WE HAVE no time
in Ireland for a man
who doesn't waste
both his money and
his time.

**STANDFORD AND
MACDOWELL, MAHAFFY**

March 29

THE POTATO after all is a wonderful root, that can rear, invigorate, and throw such life, elasticity, and energy into the human frame.

CAESAR OTWAY

October 20

Bold O'Donohue

STONES IN Killarney
Tell tales
Oft forgotten under
   the moss

Which way to the sea
O'Donohue

Oh, proud King
Whose bound feet
never
carried
him
away

MARTIN RUSSELL

March 30

WHEN EASTER arrives, we'll have mirth and revelry
Eating and drinking, and sport, and play,
Beautiful flowers, and trees, and foliage,
Dew on the grass through the live-long day.

BLIND ANTHONY RAFTERY

October 19

IN A twilight of fireside tellings
Lit by the poet's lay,
Lighting the gloom of hardship,
The night of a needy day.

STEPHEN GWYNN

March 31

THERE'S NOTHING half so sweet in life
As love's young dream.

THOMAS MOORE

October 18

THERE IS no
fireside like your
own fireside.

IRISH PROVERB

April 1

THE IRISH are a fair
people; they never
speak well of one
another.

SAMUEL JOHNSON

October 17

LITTLE CHILD, I call thee fair,
Clad in hair of golden hue,
Every lock in ringlets falling
Down, to almost kiss the dew.

DOUGLAS HYDE

April 2

The Return

For, now returned from
  golden lands,
I see Night lift her misty shroud,
And through the veil of
  morning cloud
The sun strikes northern sands;

I hail with joy the early ray
That gleams o'er valleys thrice
  more dear,

My pulse beats quicker as I hear
Up from Killiney Bay.

The whisper of familiar rills;
And sudden tremors veil
  mine eyes
As, at a turn, before me rise
Long sought, the Wicklow Hills.

George Arthur Greene

October 16

IF YE'LL GIVE me lave to light me pipe, sir,
I can tell ye something that'll divart ye.

SOPHIE MACINTOSH

April 3

WHEN APRIL rains make flowers bloom
And Johnny-jump-ups come to light,
And clouds of color and perfume
Float from the orchards pink and white,
I see my shamrock in the rain,
An emerald spray with raindrops set,
Like jewels on Spring's coronet,
So fair, and yet it breathes of pain.

MAURICE F. EGAN

October 15

I KNIT BESIDE the turf fire, I spin upon the wheel,
Winter nights for thinkin' long, round runs the reel . . .
But he never knew, he never knew that here for him
   I'd kneel.
Sparkle o' the fire,
Sparkle o' the fire,
Mother Mary, keep my love, an' send me my desire!

MOIRA O'NEILL

April 4

ONCE IN their unconstrained, after-dinner chat, Curran exclaimed to the Friar, "Reverend Father, I wish you were St. Peter."

"And why so, Counselor?"

"Because, being master of the keys, you might let me in."

"I declare to you, that it were better for you if I had the keys of the other place in my possession, for then I could let you out."

ARTHUR O'LEARY

October 14

The Wind on the Hills

GO NOT to the hills of Erin
When the night winds are about;
Put up your bar and shutter,
And so keep the danger out.

For the good-folk whirl within it,
And they pull you by the hand,
And they push you on the shoulder,
Till you move to their command.

MRS. CLEMENT SHORTER

April 5

IT WAS on that Sunday I gave my love to you; the Sunday that is last before Easter Sunday. And myself on my knees reading the Passion; and my two eyes giving love to you for ever.

BLIND ANTHONY RAFTERY

October 13

ANYBODY CAN sympathise with the sufferings of a friend, but it requires a very fine nature to sympathise with a friend's success.

OSCAR WILDE, *THE SOUL OF MAN UNDER SOCIALISM*

April 6

THREE THINGS one should do every year—listen to a storyteller at a fireside, give a hand in a corn harvest field, and climb an Irish mountain.

MICHAEL JOHN MURPHY, *MOUNTAIN YEAR*

October 12

The Gates of Dreamland

IT'S A LONELY road through bogland to the lake at Carrowmore,
And a sleeper there lies dreaming where the water laps
   the shore.
Though the moth-wings of the twilight in their purples
   are unfurled
Yet his sleep is filled with gold light by the masters
   of the world.

GEORGE W. RUSSELL

April 7

Epitaph on Edward Purdon

HERE LIES poor Ned Purdon, from misery freed,
Who long was a bookseller's hack;
He led such a damnable life in this world,—
I don't think he'll wish to come back.

OLIVER GOLDSMITH

October 11

CHILDREN ARE the world's greatest resource and our best hope for the future.

REV. JIM CLOSE, PRESIDENT OF THE MERCY HOME FOR BOYS AND GIRLS

April 8

Roman View of Ireland

BEYOND BRITAIN lies Iuvernia, an island of nearly equal size, but oblong, and a coast on each side of equal extent, having a climate unfavourable for ripening grain, but so luxuriant in grasses, not merely palatable but even sweet, that the cattle in very short time take sufficient food for the whole day— and if fed too long, would burst.

POMPONIUS MELA (1ST CENTURY)

October 10

A MAN, WEARY after a long walk, asked a peasant whom he met on the high road how far he was from a certain village. "Just four short miles," was the reply. Now the place happened to be eight miles distant, and the peasant was aware of the fact. Why, then, did he deceive the man? "Shure," said he, when reproved for the deception, "I saw the poor fellow was tired, and I wanted to keep his courage up."

MICHAEL MACDONAGH

April 9

FOR FAITHFUL is an Irishman.

JAMES ORR

October 9

IT IS far and it is far
To Connemara where you are,
To where its purple glens enfold you
As glowing heavens that hold a star.

And we shall be, we yet shall be
Oh Colleen lonely, beloved by me,
For evermore on a moor of Mayo,
Mid heather singing like the sea.

ALICE MILLIGAN

April 10

THEY THOUGHT I was doing outside public relations. I was simply going from bar to bar.

MALACHY MCCOURT, AUTHOR/PLAYWRIGHT

October 8

WHEN YOUR hand is
in the dog's mouth,
draw it out gently.

IRISH PROVERB

April 11

O HEART, IF you sing not while we are together,
What man shall remember my love or me?

ARTHUR O'SHAUGHNESSY

October 7

HEALTH AND long life to you.
The wife (or husband) of your choice to you.
A child every year to you.
Land without rent to you.
And may you be half-an-hour in heaven
before the devil knows you're dead.

IRISH TOAST

April 12

The Low-Backed Car

WHEN I first met sweet Peggy,
'Twas on a market day,
A low-backed car she drove, and sat
Upon a truss of hay.
But when that hay was blooming grass,
And decked with flowers of spring,
No flower was there that could compare
With the blooming girl I sing.

SAMUEL LOVER

October 6

EVERY MAN desires to
live long; but no
man would be old.

JONATHAN SWIFT

April 13

An old castle towers o'er
the billow
That thunders by Cleena's
green land,
And there dwelt as gallant a
rover
As ever grasped hilt by the hand.
Eight stately towers of the
waters
Lie anchored in Baltimore Bay,
And over their twenty
score sailors,
Oh! who but the Rover
holds sway?
Then, ho! For Fineen the Rover!
Fineen O'Driscoll the free!
Straight as the mast of his galley,
And wild as the wave of
the sea!

ROBERT DWYER JOYCE

October 5

Feithfailge

THE BLUE lake of Devenish!
I put my thousand blessings
there;
(The blue lake of Devenish)
On shadow waters all a-stir,
And on the wind-blown
honeysuckle
Beauty of Feithfailge's hair.

The blue lake of Devenish!
I pray, if God but grant the
grace,
(The blue lake of Devenish,)
To win that dear enchanted
place,
Where spring bides in the
apple-blossom,
Beauty of Feithfailge's face.

ETHNA CARBERRY

April 14

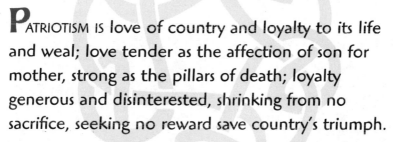

PATRIOTISM IS love of country and loyalty to its life and weal; love tender as the affection of son for mother, strong as the pillars of death; loyalty generous and disinterested, shrinking from no sacrifice, seeking no reward save country's triumph.

ARCHBISHOP JOHN IRELAND

October 4

OUR HEARTS and our liquors are stout.

OLIVER GOLDSMITH

April 15

⊗

MAY GOOD luck be with you
Wherever you go,
And your blessings outnumber
The shamrocks that grow.

IRISH BLESSING

October 3

GOD OF the winds! oh hear my prayer!
Safe passage now bestow!
Soft o'er the slumbering deep, may fair
And prosperous breezes flow!
O'er the rough rock and swelling wave,
Do thou our progress guide!
Do thou from angry ocean save,
And o'er its rage preside!

CHARLOTTE BROOKE

April 16

IF YOU encounter a black dog with blazing red eyes, quickly make the sign of the cross. The dog will leap in the air and disappear, for it is merely the devil in disguise.

October 2

WE MUST make
students understand
that Ireland does not
exist in a vacuum.

EAMONN WALL,
POET AND DIRECTOR OF IRISH STUDIES,
CREIGHTON UNIVERSITY

April 17

RIVER OF billows, to whose mighty heart
The tide-wave rushes of the Atlantic Sea;
River of quiet depths, by culturead lea,
Romantic wood or city's crowded mart;
River of old poetic founts, which start
From their lone mountain-cradles, wild and free,
Nursed with the fawns, lulled by the woodlark's glee...

SIR AUBREY DE VERE

October 1

He that goes to bed, and goes to bed sober,
Falls as the leaves do, falls as the leaves do,
   and dies in October;
But he that goes to bed, and goes to bed mellow,
Lives as he ought to do, lives as he ought to do,
   and dies an honest fellow.

Maria Edgeworth

April 18

The Fair Hills of Ireland

A PLENTEOUS PLACE is Ireland for hospitable cheer,
Uileacán dubh O!
Where the wholesome fruit is bursting from the yellow barley ear;
There is honey in the trees where her misty vales expand,
And her forest paths, in summer, are by falling waters fanned;
There is dew at high noontide there,
   and springs in the yellow sand,
On the fair hills of holy Ireland.

JOHN COLLINS

September 30

MY LIFE is like the autumn leaf,
That trembles in the moon's pale ray,
Its hold is frail—its date is brief,
Restless—and soon to pass away!
Yet, ere that leaf shall fall and fade,
The parent tree will mourn its shade,
The winds bewail the leafless tree,
But none shall breathe a sigh for me!

RICHARD HENRY WILDE

April 19

AN OLD broom
knows the dirty
corners best.

IRISH PROVERB

September 29

BRIAN O'LINN was a gentleman born,
His hair it was long and his beard unshorn,
His teeth were out and his eyes far in—
"I'm a wonderful beauty," says Brian O'Linn!

JOHN HAND

April 20

MAN IS born a social being.

ARCHBISHOP JOHN IRELAND

September 28

HE'S HALF an hour late,
While here I wait and wait.
Well, it is just my fate—
Too plainly I can see,
He never cared for me.
How cruel men can be!

FRANCES WYNNE

April 21

I SAT WITHIN the valley green,
I sat me with my true love;
My sad heart strove the two between,
The old love and the new love;
The old for her, the new that made
Me think on Ireland dearly,
When soft the wind blew down the glade,
And shook the golden barley.

ROBERT DWYER JOYCE

September 27

TWO YOUNG ladies stopped to talk to an old man working in a potato field. In the course of the conversation one said to him, "Which of us do you think is the elder?" "Ah, thin, each of ye looks younger than the other," replied the gallant old fellow.

MICHAEL MACDONAGH

April 22

THERE'S MANY a dry eye at a moneylender's funeral.

A CORK RESIDENT

September 26

THE TIME I've lost in wooing,
In watching and pursuing
The light that lies
In woman's eyes,
Has been my heart's undoing.
Though Wisdom oft has sought me,
I scorned the lore she brought me,
My only books
Were woman's looks
And folly's all they've taught me.

THOMAS MOORE

April 23

⊗

WHEN I had mounted the white steed, he galloped straight towards the shore. We moved as swiftly as before over the clear sea. The wind overtook the waves and we overtook the wind, so that we straightway left the Land of Youth behind; and we passed by many islands and cities, till at length we landed on the green shores of Erin.

PATRICK WESTON JOYCE

September 25

WHEN BIRDS are silent
and oxen drowse
Why should a maiden spin?

LADY GILBERT

April 24

The Scalp

STERN GRANITE Gate of Wicklow, with what awe,
What triumph, oft (glad children strayed from home)
We passed into thy shadows cool, to roam
The Land beyond, whose very name could draw
A radiance to our faces; till we saw,
With airy peak and purple mountain-dome,
And lawn and wood and blue bay flecked with foam,
The Land indeed—fair truth without one flaw!

GEORGE FRANCIS SAVAGE-ARMSTRONG

September 24

IF YOU get one
good line a day,
you're doing well.

BILLY ROCHE, IRISH PLAYWRIGHT

April 25

MAY THE roof above
us never fall in, and may
we friends gathered
below never fall out.

IRISH TOAST

September 23

NOW MEMORY, false, spendthrift Memory,
Disloyal treasure-keeper of the soul...

STANDISH O'GRADY

April 26

A-SOUTH, BEYOND the hamlet, lie
The low, blue hills in mingling mist,
Wirth furl of cloud along the sky,
And ravines rich as amethyst,
And mellow edges gold-ored
As sinks the round sun in the flood,
And high up wings the crow line toward
Old turrets in the distant wood...

THOMAS CAULFIELD IRWIN

September 22

MAY THE lilt of Irish laughter
Lighten every load,
May the mist of Irish magic
Shorten every road,
May you taste the sweetest pleasures
That fortune ere bestowed,
And may all your friends remember
All the favors you are owed.

IRISH BLESSING

April 27

THE BRAINS and tongues of the Irish are somehow differently formed or furnished from those of other people.

SIR JONAH BARRINGTON,
PERSONAL SKETCHES

September 21

FOLLOW, FOLLOW, follow, follow,
Follow, follow pleasure—
There's no drinking in the grave.

GEORGE OGLE

April 28

I HAVE KNOWN several persons of great fame for wisdom in public affairs and counsels, governed by foolish servants.

JONATHAN SWIFT

September 20

A LITTLE LONELY moorland lake,
Its waters brown and cool and deep—
The cliff, the hills behind it make
A picture for my heart to keep.

ROSE KAVANAGH

April 29

HERE THE first daisies break free from the sod,
Stars looking up with their first glance to God!
Here, ere the first days of April are done,
Stand the swart cherry trees robed with the sun;
In the deep woodland the windflowers blow;
Where young grass is springing, the crocuses glow,
Down the green glen is the primrose's light,
Soft shines the hawthorn's raiment of white;
Round the rough knees of the crabtree a ring
Of daffodils dance for joy of the spring...

ROSE KAVANAGH

September 19

I ONCE MET an old peasant who had married when he was nineteen and thought he had not done well. "I'll niver marry again so young if I wor to live to the age of Methuselah!" he exclaimed. And he kept his word; he was eighty when he married the second time.

MICHAEL MACDONAGH

April 30

'TWAS THUS, as under shade I stood,
I sung my wishes to the wood,
And lost in thought, no more perceived
The branches whisper as they waved...

THOMAS PARNELL

September 18

BUT MORN is blushing in the sky.

THOMAS MOORE

May 1

Hot Time

NAMED AFTER the god Bel, Beltane is derived from the god's name and the word *tan*, meaning "fire." In this spring festival, traditionally celebrated on May 1, cattle herds are driven through two ceremonial fires as a purification ritual as the winter darkness lifts.

September 17

A PLEASANT LAND of
winding vales, bright
streams, and verdurous
plains,
Where summer all the live-
long year in changeless
splendor reigns,
A peaceful land of calm
delight, of everlasting
bloom;

Old age and death we never
know, no sickness, care,
or gloom;
The land of youth,
Of love and truth,
From pain and sorrow free,
The land of rest,
In the golden west,
On the verge of the azure
sea!

PATRICK WESTON JOYCE

May 2

ONCE IN the Maytime your carol so sweet
Found out my heart in the midst of the street.
Ah! how I listened, and you murmured low
Hope, wide as earth and as white as the snow;
Hope that, alas! like the foam on your breast,
Broke and was drifted away from its rest.

ROSE KAVANAGH

September 16

OF ALL climates, Ireland is the most temperate. Neither extraordinary heat in summer is felt there, nor excessive cold in winter. That country is so blessed in these particulars, that it seems as if nature looked upon it with a more favorable eye than on any other.

JOHN MITCHEL

May 3

Full House

LEAP CASTLE in County Offaly is reported to house more haunts than any other castle in Ireland, with 24 ghosts rattling through its ancient halls.

September 15

The Critic

THE POET proclaimed himself of epic proportions,
Undaunted,
As he perched on the stool and read

Flannery, he in the back row, slowly rose
Like the King of Leinster, he was, shaking his fist
And demanding restitution for having to sit
   through it all

MARTIN RUSSELL

May 4

A WELL-FOUND boat, four springing oars set in motion by as elastic backs, soon brought us in the middle of the bay of Skull; not a breath was on the ocean; the gray mist of the morning had risen, and was dissolved in the clear cold atmosphere; the sun walked above in its pride of light, the harbor had become a looking glass for the hills and headlands to dress themselves in, and assume a softer and sweeter countenance ...

CAESAR OTWAY

September 14

The Wild Geese

WHEN THE wintry frosts begin,
And in their long drawn lonely flight
The wild geese with their airy din
Distend the ear of night.

SIR SAMUEL FERGUSON

May 5

My Mother Dear

THERE WAS a place in childhood that I remember well,
And there a voice of sweetest tone bright fairy-tales did tell,
And gentle words and fond embrace were giv'n with
    joy to me,
When I was in that happy place—upon my mother's knee.

SAMUEL LOVER

September 13

WITHIN THE windows of
    this white
Low, ivy-roofed, retired abode,
We look through sunset's
    sinking light
Along the lone and dusty road
That leads unto the river's
    bridge,
Where stand two sycamores
    broad and green,

Whence from their rising
    grassy ridge
The low rays lengthen shade
    and sheen.
The village panes reflect
    the glow,
And all about the scene is still,
Save, by the foamy dam below,
The drumming wheel of the
    whitewashed mill.

THOMAS CAULFIELD IRWIN

May 6

O HEART FULL of song in the sweet song-weather,
A voice fills each bower, a wing shakes each tree,
Come forth, O winged singer, on song's fairest feather,
And make a sweet fame of my love and of me.

The blithe world shall ever have fair loving leisure,
And long in the summer for bird and for bee;
But too short the summer and too keen the pleasure
Of me kissing her and of her kissing me.

ARTHUR O'SHAUGHNESSY

September 12

THE MEN in Northern Ireland are not the easiest to talk with, God knows. But I think I have to say that I'm probably not one of the easiest women they've had to talk to . . . I swear a lot . . . .

**MAJORIE (MO) MOWLAM,
NORTHERN IRELAND SECRETARY OF STATE**

May 7

LET'S HAVE mirth while time we have...

GEORGE OGLE

September 11

THE GRAY mist of morning in autumn was fleeting,
When I met the bright darling down in the boreen;
Her words were unkind, but I soon won a greeting;
Sweet kisses I stole from the lips of Brideen!

Then shine, O bright Sun, on thy constant, true lover;
Then shine once again in the leafy boreen,
And the clouds shall depart that around my heart hover,
And we'll walk amid gladness, my gentle Brideen!

GEORGE SIGERSON

May 8

ARRAH! BRIGID MacSheehy, your eyes are the death
  o' me,
And your laugh, like a fairy stroke, knocks out the breath
  o' me!
The devil a cobweb of slumber, till dawned the day,
Has come to my lids, while the long night I yawned away!
Och, you heart-killing imp, 't was your witchery puzzled me;
Like a bird by a night-wisp, your beauty has dazzled me!

MICHAEL HOGAN

September 10

❊

ALL THAT philosophy can teach is to be stubborn or sullen under misfortunes.

OLIVER GOLDSMITH

May 9

THE JEWEL most rare is the jewel most fair.

IRISH PROVERB

September 9

What Will You Do, Love?

WHAT WILL you do, love,
    when I am going,
With white sail flowing,
The seas beyond?—
What will you do, love,
    when waves divide us,
And friends may chide us
For being fond?

Though waves divide us, and
    friends be chiding,
In faith abiding,
I'll still be true!
And I'll pray for thee on the
    stormy ocean,
In deep devotion—
That's what I'll do!

SAMUEL LOVER

May 10

THERE'S A colleen fair as May,
For a year and for a day
I've sought by every way—Her heart to gain.
There's no art of tongue or eye,
Fond youths with maidens try,
But I've tried with ceaseless sigh—Yet tried in vain.

GEORGE PETRIE

September 8

ANY PLACE with
stout on tap can't
be all that bad.

MALCOLM MCDOWELL WOODS,
JOURNALIST

May 11

IT WAS the general rule of every man, in the character of a gentleman, never to gallop or even trot hard upon a road, except emergency required haste.

JOHN O'KEEFE

September 7

Animal Story

ST. MULLEN of Carlow loved animals so much that he not only rescued a wren that had been swallowed by a cat, but also rescued a fly that had been swallowed by the wren.

May 12

SHE IS a rich and rare land;
O she's a fresh and fair land;
She is a dear and rare land—
This native land of mine.

No men than hers are
    braver—
Her women's hearts ne'er
    waver;

I'd freely die to save her,
And think my lot divine.

She's not a dull or cold land;
No! she's a warm and bold
    land;
O she's a true and old land—
This native land of mine.

THOMAS OSBORNE DAVIS

September 6

Nationality

EACH NATION master at its own fireside—
The claim is just, and so one day 't will be;
But a wise race the time of fruit will bide,
Nor pluck th' unripened apple from the tree.

JOHN KELLS INGRAM

May 13

Sure this is blessed Erin an' this the same glen,
The gold is on the whin-bush, the wather
   sings again,
The Fairy Thorn's in flower,—an' what ails my
   heart then?
Flower o' the May,
Flower o' the May,
What about May time, an' he far away!

Moira O'Neill

September 5

Very Far Away

O SHIP! O sail! far must ye be
Ere gleams like that upon ye light.
O'er golden spaces of the sea,
From mysteries of the lucent night,
Such touch comes never to the boat
Wherein across waves we float.

WILLIAM ALEXANDER

May 14

FROM THE day you marry, your heart will be in your mouth and your hand in your pocket.

IRISH PROVERB

September 4

MORALLY, THE general superiority of women over man is, I think, unquestionable.

WILLIAM E. H. LECKY

May 15

WHEN PADDY heard an English gentleman speaking of the fine echo at the lake of Killarney, which repeats the sound forty times, he very promptly observed: "Faith, that's nothing at all to the echo in my father's garden, in the county of Galway: if you say to it, 'How do you do, Paddy Blake?' it will answer, 'Pretty well, I thank you, sir.'"

MARIA EDGEWORTH

September 3

THE SOIL is rich and soft,
   the air is mild and bland,
Of the fair hills of Eiré O!

DONOGH MAC CON-MARA

May 16

Lovely Mary Donnelly

WHEN SHE stood up for dancing, her steps were so complete,
The music nearly killed itself to listen to her feet;
The fiddler moaned his blindness, he heard her so much praised,
But blessed his luck to not be deaf when once her voice she raised.

WILLIAM ALLINGHAM

September 2

In September

WHERE LURK the merry elves of Autumn now,
In this bright breezy month of equinox?
Among tanned bracken on the mountain's brow;
Or deep in heather tufted round white rocks
On a wild moor, where heath-bells wither slow,
Twined with late blooming furze—a home of grouse?
By river alders? Or on stubbly plains?
Bound not their kingdom so;
They follow Beauty's train, of all her house
Gay pensioners, till not one leaf remains.

JOHN TODHUNTER

May 17

THE SAVAGE loves his native shore,
Though rude the soil and chill the air;
Then well may Erin's sons adore
Their isle, which nature formed so fair.
What flood reflects a shore so sweet
As Shannon great, or pastoral Bann?
Or who a friend or foe can meet
So generous as an Irishman?

JAMES ORR

September 1

A TROUT IN the pot is better than a salmon in the sea.

IRISH PROVERB

May 18

It is a custom amongst the people, when throwing away water at night, to cry out in a loud voice, "Take care of the water;" or literally, from the Irish, "Away with yourself from the water"—for they say that the spirits of the dead last buried are then wandering about, and it would be dangerous if the water fell on them.

LADY WILDE

August 31

LET ME join with you the jubilant procession,
Let me chant with you her story;
Then contented I shall go back to the shamrocks,
Now mine eyes have seen her glory.

FANNY PARNELL

May 19

❈

The Flitting of the Fairies

RED-ROSE mists o'erdrift
Moth-moon's glimmering white,
Lit by sheen-silled west
Barred with fiery bar;
Fleeting, following swift,
Whither across the night
Seek we bourne of rest?

JANE BARLOW

August 30

THE THEATER is a great healer.

MAGGIE CRONIN, BELFAST ACTRESS

May 20

THE HEART that
has truly loved
never forgets.

THOMAS MOORE

August 29

THE WORK that should to-day be wrought,
Defer not till to-morrow;
The help that should within be sought,
Scorn from without to borrow.
Old maxims these—yet stout and true—
They speak in trumpet tone,
To do at once what is to do,
And trust OURSELVES ALONE.

JOHN O'HAGAN

May 21

The Dawning of the Day

AT THE early dawn I once had been
Where Lene's blue waters flow,
When summer bid the groves be green,
The lamp of light to glow.
As on by bower, and town, and tower,
And widespread fields I stray,
I met a maid in the greenwood shade
At the dawning of the day.

EDWARD WALSH

August 28

IT IS not in fighting that my God delights but in causing the trees to grow, and in adorning the plains with grass and flowers. He loves not the proud warrior nor the hunter, but the lowly and the good.

STANDISH O'GRADY

May 22

THE MISTS of age
May make these summer seasons dim . . .

THOMAS CAULFIELD IRWIN

August 27

Dear Harp of my Country! in darkness I found thee,
The cold chain of silence had hung o'er thee long,
When proudly, my own Island Harp, I unbound thee,
And gave all thy chords to light, freedom, and song!

Thomas Moore

May 23

Fairy Gold

BUTTERCUPS AND daisies in the meadow,
And the children pick them as they pass,
Weaving in the sunlight and the shadow
Garlands for each little lad and lass;
Weave with dreams their buttercups and daisies,
As the poor dead children did of old.
Will the dreams, like sunshine in their faces,
Wither with their flowers like Fairy Gold?

JOHN TODHUNTER

August 26

COME IN the evening, or come in the morning.
Come where you're looked for, or come without
   warning;
Kisses and welcome you'll have here before ye.
And the oftener you come here the more
   I'll adore ye.

JOHN HAND

May 24

OH FAME! Fame! you incorrigible gossip!

JAMES KENNEY

August 25

I LIVE A **non-journalist's life.
I look for the texture of
ordinary things.**

NUALA O'FAOLAIN, COLUMNIST/AUTHOR

May 25

SWEET, THERE is nothing left to say
But this, that love is never lost,
Keen winter stabs the breasts of May
Whose crimson roses burst his frost,
Ships tempest-tossed
Will find a harbor in some bay,
And so we may.

OSCAR WILDE

August 24

YOU SAUCY south wind, setting
all the budded beech boughs
swinging
Above the wood anemones that
flutter, flushed and white,
When far across the wide salt
waves your quick way you
were winging,
Oh! tell me, tell me, did you
pass my sweetheart's ship last
night?
Ah! let the daisies be,
South wind, and answer me:
Did you my sailor see?
Wind, whisper very low,
For none but you must know
I love my lover so.

FRANCES WYNNE

May 26

PATRIOTISM! There is
magic in the word.
It is bliss to repeat it.
ARCHBISHOP JOHN IRELAND

August 23

YOU SEE, my good friend, how much we are the creatures of situation and circumstance, and with what pliant servility the mind resigns itself to the impressions of the senses, or the illusions of the imagination.

LADY MORGAN

May 27

NEVER BEFORE or since, in Ireland, did the summer sun dart fiercer rays than, as if in sympathy with the passions and acts it witnessed, during the hot struggle of civil war in the year 1798.

MICHAEL BANIM

August 22

Among the Heather

Your MOUNTAIN air is sweet when the days are
   long and sunny.
When the grass grows round the rocks, and the whin-bloom
   smells like honey.
But the winter's coming fast with its foggy, snowy weather,
And you'll find it bleak and chill on your hill among
   the heather.

WILLIAM ALLINGHAM

May 28

The Lover and the Birds

"There's something, something sad,
I half remember," piped a broken strain;
Well sung, sweet Robin! Robin, sing again.
"Spring's opening cheerily, cheerily! be we glad!"
Which moved, I wist not why, me melancholy mad,
Till now, grown meek,
With wetted cheek,
Most comforting and gentle thoughts I had.

WILLIAM ALLINGHAM

August 21

Politics is not my domain.
Charity, and charity alone,
is my obsession.

Sister Consuelo Murphy,
Irish missionary

May 29

I SELL MY work by the quality, not the quantity.

CHARLES JOHNSTONE

August 20

Whene're I see soft hazel eyes,
And nut-brown curls,
I think of those bright days I spent
Among the Limerick girls;
When up through Cratla woods I went
Nutting with thee;
And we plucked the glossy, clustering fruit
From many a bending tree.

SIR SAMUEL FERGUSON

May 30

THE YOUNG May moon is beaming, love,
The glowworm's lamp is gleaming, love,
How sweet to rove
Through Morna's grove,
While the drowsy world is dreaming, love!
Then awake!—the heavens look bright, my dear!
'T is never too late for delight, my dear!
And the best of all ways
To lengthen our days
Is to steal a few hours from the night, my dear!

THOMAS MOORE

August 19

AGE AND knowledge only contribute to sour our dispositions.

OLIVER GOLDSMITH

May 31

A LARGE ADVANCE creates motivation
like nothing else.

MALACHY McCOURT, AUTHOR/PLAYWRIGHT

August 18

The Earth and Man

A LITTLE SUN, a little rain,
A soft wind blowing from the west,
And woods and fields are sweet again,
And warmth within the mountain's breast.

So simple is the earth we tread,
So quick with love and life her frame,
Ten thousand years have dawned and fled
And still her magic is the same.

STOPFORD AUGUSTUS BROOKE

June 1

Longing

O THE SUNSHINE of old
   Ireland, when it lies
On her woods and on
   her waters;
And gleams through
   her soft skies,
Tenderly as the lovelight in
   her daughters'
Gentle eyes!

O the brown streams of old
   Ireland, how they leap
From her glens, and fill
   their hollows
With wild songs, till charmed
   to sleep
By the murmuring bees in
   meadows, where the swallows
Glance and sweep!

JOHN TODHUNTER

August 17

THE DEWDROPS lie bright mid
the grass and yellow corn
On the fair hills of Eiré O!

DONOGH MAC CON-MARA

June 2

A ROSE, YOU see, is known the wide world over, and so is a thistle; but there is great danger of a man's mistaking a clover for a shamrock.

ELSA D'ESTERRE-KEELING

August 16

POVERTY WAS a permanent
feature in our home.
We did not always live in
a slum, we only moved in
when we could afford it.

ART MCMILLEN, BELFAST RESIDENT

June 3

To My Bicycle

IN THE airy whirling wheel is the springing strength of steel,
And the sinew grows to steel day by day,
Till you feel your pulses leap at the easy swing and sweep
As the hedges flicker past upon your way.
Then it's out to the kiss of the morning breeze
And the rose of the morning sky,
And the long brown road where the tired spirit's load
Slips off as the leagues go by!

THOMAS W. HAZEN ROLLESTON

August 15

Saintly Cuisine

ATCHEN WAS a lad who prepared meals for St. Patrick. Patrick later made him bishop of Bodony in Tyrone. Subsequently, Atchen has become the patron saint of Irish cookery, and many dishes have been named in his honor.

June 4

How can there be too much Irishness.

Tom Bruno, theater professor

August 14

IRELAND IS a small but insuppressible island half an hour nearer the sunset than Great Britain.

THOMAS KETTLE, "ON CROSSING THE IRISH SEA"

June 5

MY LIFE is like the summer rose,
That opens to the morning sky,
But ere the shades of evening close,
Is scattered on the ground—to die.
Yet on the rose's humble bed
The sweetest dews of night are shed,
As if she wept the waste to see—
But none shall weep a tear for me!

RICHARD HENRY WILDE

August 13

COME ALL you pale lovers that sigh and complain,
While your beautiful tyrants but laugh at your pain,
Come practice with me
To be happy and free,
In spite of inconstancy, pride, or disdain.
I see and I love, and the bliss I enjoy
No rival can lessen nor envy destroy.

THOMAS DUFFET

June 6

I'VE HEARD the lark in June,
The harp's wild plaintive tune,
The thrush, that aye too soon
Gives o'er his strain—
I've heard in hushed delight,
The mellow horn at night,
Waking the echoes light
Of old Loch Lene;
But neither echoing horn,
Nor thrush upon the thorn,

Nor lark at early morn,
Hymning in air,
Nor harper's lay divine,
E'er witched this heart
    of mine,
Like that sweet voice
    of thine,
That ev'ning there.

DENNY LANE

August 12

I F ST. PATRICK had been asked to designate a "purgatory" for Ireland, Lough Derg would fit the bill perfectly. Not because it's deary—nothing in scenic Ireland could be—but because you have to talk in whispers there. What could be more cruel for a nation blessed with the gift of gab! Some might even call it "hell."

LORRAINE O'DONNELL WILLIAM
(DESCRIBING A MONASTRY IN DONEGAL)

June 7

THE IRISH underworld has no morals but a strong sense of economics.

DECLAN HUGHES, PLAYWRIGHT

August 11

Take the Shannon Way

Take the Shannon Way, she says
Black eyes run through my soul

Take the Shannon Way,
    past the swans
Hand waves toward the
    moon-encrusted sea

Flee to the night, she says
Mothlike fingers touch my eyes

The Shannon has dampened

God's sleeve, she says
Steaming hair captured by the
    wind, red lips . . . wanting

Go now, before the spider
    works its tapestry
Wind-chime voices tiptoe on
    the water's mirror

Calling . . .

MARTIN RUSSELL

June 8

LEAVE THE flurry
To the masses;
Take your time
And shine your glasses.

OLD IRISH VERSE

August 10

I SEE AN envied haunt of peace,
Calm and untouched; remote from roar,
Where wearied men may from their burdens cease
On a still shore.

EMILY LAWLESS

June 9

I WATCHED LAST night the rising moon
Upon a foreign strand,
Till memories came, like flowers of June,
Of home and fatherland;
I dreamt I was a child once more
Beside the rippling rill,
Where first I saw in days of yore
The moon behind the hill.

WILLIAM KENEALY

August 9

Women are intellectually more desultory and volatile than men; they are more occupied with particular instances than with general principles; they judge rather by intuitive perceptions than by deliberate reasoning or past experience. They are, however, usually superior to men in nimbleness and rapidity of thought, and in the gift of tact or the power of seizing speedily and faithfully the finer inflections of feeling; and they have therefore often attained very great eminence in conversation, as letterwriters, as actresses, and as novelists.

William E. H. Lecky

June 10

FOR MEMORY loves on wine to float.

THOMAS CAULFIELD IRWIN

August 8

THESE THINGS I warmly wish for you—
Someone to love,
Some work to do, A bit o' sun
A bit o' cheer
And a guardian angel
Always near.

OLD IRISH GREETING

June 11

THE GLOOM of the sea-fronting cliffs
Lay on the water, violet-dark;
The pennon dropped, the sail fell in,
And slowly moved our bark.

A golden day; the summer dreamed
In heaven and on the whispering sea,
Within our hearts the summer dreamed;
The hours had ceased to be.

EDWARD DOWDEN

August 7

LEARNING IS better than house or land.

MARIA EDGEWORTH

June 12

SATIRE MUST be
personal, or it
will never do.

CHARLES JOHNSTONE

August 6

THE SWAN upon the lake,
The wild rose in the break,
The golden clouds that make
The west their throne,
The wild ash by the stream,
The full moon's silver beam,
The ev'ning star's soft gleam,
Shining alone;

The lily robed in white,
All, all are fair and bright;
But ne'er on earth was sight
So bright, so fair,
As that one glimpse of thee,
That I caught then, machree,
It stole my heart from me
That ev'ning there.

DENNY LANE

June 13

As the white low mist the meadows kissed
In the summer twilight's glow,
And the otter splashed and the wild duck dashed
In the sedgy lake below.
'Twas sweet to hear the silver bell
For the flocks on high Dunroe.

WILLIAM CARLETON

August 5

THERE'S MANY'S the thing a man sez, that he doesn't do.

CHARLOTTE O'CONOR ECCLES

June 14

LET YOUR anger set with the sun
and not rise again with it.

IRISH PROVERB

August 4

I LOVE YOU, and I love you, and I love you,
   O my honey!
It isn't for your goodly lands, it isn't for your money;
It isn't for your father's cows, your mother's
   yellow butter,
The love that's in my heart for you no words of
   mine may utter!

MARY FURLONG

June 15

NOW IN the lonely hour when with her ray
The moon o'er ocean trailed a shimmering way
That the bright Spirit-folk to heaven might take,
A voice struck Naisi's ear and bade him wake.

ROBERT DWYER JOYCE

August 3

SOME MEN, under the notions of weeding out prejudices, eradicate virtue, honesty, and religion.

JONATHAN SWIFT

June 16

O THE BROOM banks of the river are fair,
Now the wild brier is blossoming there—
Now when the green banks so calmly repose,
Lulled by the river's strange chant as it goes,
Laughing beneath the gold eyes of the broom,
Flashing so free whure the heather's in bloom,
Blushing all o'er at the kiss of the sun,
Tranquil again at the gaze of a nun.
Is it, my river, a sob or a song
Beats from that heart as you hurry along?

ROSE KAVANAGH

August 2

Erin to Her Own Tune

WHEN ERIN first rose from the dark-swelling flood,
God blessed the green island, he saw it was good.
The Emerald of Europe, it sparkled and shone
In the ring of this world, the most precious stone.

June 17

STILL LET my thoughts,
    leaving the worldly roar
Like pilgrims, wander on
    thy haunted shore.

STANDISH O'GRADY

August 1

WHEN AN artist goes to sketch in the West of Ireland, there is often trouble in getting a suitable place to stay. There are lodgings that advertise bed and board for five shillings, but you can't tell very often which is the bed and which is the board.

PERCY FRENCH, *MY FRIEND FINNEGAN*

June 18

O *DONALL OG*, if you go across the sea, bring myself with you and do not forget it; and you will have a sweetheart for fair days and market days, and the daughter of the King of Greece beside you at night.

It is late last night the dog was speaking of you; the snipe was speaking of you in her deep marsh. It is you are the lonely bird through the woods; and that you may be without a mate until you find me.

BLIND ANTHONY RAFTERY

July 31

THERE'S MUSIC there
And all kinds of
 sweetness
In the piper's
 greeting
At the end of day...

June 19

I'LL PURCHASE the best wedding ring in the town for you!
Or by thunder, to make one I'll pull the moon down for you!
If I could lay my hand on the sun for a crown for you,
Sure, I'd be the boy that would win light and renown for you!
Now, Biddy, my jewel! what have you to say to me?
Just give up your heart without further delay to me;
And I will bless this as a glorious fine day to me—
If a queen got such a courting, by Jove, she'd give way to me!

MICHAEL HOGAN

July 30

⊗

IF YOU would make Fortune your friend . . . if you desire, my son, to be rich, and have money, be more eager to save than acquire: when people say, Money is to be got here, and money is to be got there, take no notice; mind your own business; stay where you are, and secure all you can get, without stirring.

OLIVER GOLDSMITH

June 20

THE DEW-DROPS sparkle,
like diamonds on the corn,
Fair Hills of Firé O!

DONOGH MAC CON-MARA

July 29

No one can look over the fugitive literature of Dublin in the first half of the eighteenth century without being struck with the very large amount of admirable witty and satirical poetry that was produced.

William E. H. Lecky

June 21

OH! 'T WAS Dermot O'Nowlan McFigg.
That could properly handle a twig.
He went to the Fair,
And kicked up a dust there,
In dancing the Donnybrook Jig,
With his twig,
Oh! my blessing to Dermot McFigg!

CHARLES O'FLAHERTY

July 28

ART THOU a thing of earth?
A maid of terrestrial birth?
Or a vision sent from high
In peerless beauty beaming,
Like the shapes that pass o'er the poet's eye
When he lies all idly dreaming.

THOMAS FURLONG

June 22

IRISH CULTURE
is borderless.

LIAM LYNCH

July 27

THE JESTS of the rich are ever successful.

OLIVER GOLDSMITH

June 23

WERE YOU ever in sweet Tipperary, where the fields are
so sunny and green,
And the heath-brown Slieve-bloom and the Galtees look
down with so proud a mien?
'T is there you would see more beauty than is on all Irish
ground—
God bless you, my sweet Tipperary, for where could your
match be found?

MRS. KEVIN IZOD O'DOHERTY

July 26

O_{F ALL} trades that flourished of old,
Before men knew reading and writing,
The friars' was the best, I am told,
If one wasn't much given to fighting;
For, rent free, you lived at your ease—
You had neither to work nor to labor—
You might eat of whatever you please,
For the prog was supplied by your neighbor.
O, good luck to the friars of old!

CHARLES JAMES LEVER

June 24

MAN IS no mushroom growth of yesterday.

JOHN KELLS INGRAM

July 25

THE MOST accomplished way of using books is to serve them as some people do lords; learn their *titles* and then *brag* of their acquaintance.

LAURENCE STERNE

June 25

I KNOW A lake where the cool waves break,
And softly fall on the silver sand—
And no steps intrude on that solitude,
And no voice, save mine, disturbs the strand.

If it were my lot in that fairy spot
To live for ever, and dream 't were mine,
Courts might woo, and kings pursue,
Ere I would leave thee—Loved Loc-Ine.

FITZ JAMES O'BRIEN

July 24

DID YE hear of the widow
  Malone,
Ohone!
Who lived in the town of
  Athlone,
Alone?
Oh! She melted the hearts
Of the swains in them parts—
So lovely the widow Malone,
Ohone!
So lovely the widow Malone.

Of lovers she had a full score
Or more;
And fortunes they all had galore,
In store;
From the minister down
To the Clerk of the Crown,
All were courting the widow
  Malone,
Ohone!
All were the courting the
  widow Malone.

CHARLES JAMES LEVER

June 26

WHEN YOUTHFUL spring around us breathes,
They Spirit warms her fragrant sigh;
And every flower the summer wreathes
Is born beneath that kindling eye.
Where'er we turn, thy glories shine,
And all things fair and bright are thine.

THOMAS MOORE

July 23

IN THE heart of high blue hills
Where the silence thrills and thrills,
In the Valley of the Thrushes:
From the golden low furze-bushes
On the mountain wind's light feet
Comes a perfume faint and sweet.

MARY FURLONG

June 27

DESPITE WHAT you
have heard: Guinness
is not a meal.

MIKE DANAHY, JOURNALIST

July 22

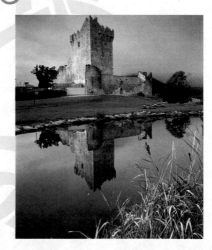

THE LOGIC of the Irish mind takes naturally, there-fore, the form of rhetoric or oratory.

HENRY GILES

June 28

Faint are the breezes, and pure is the tide,
Soft is the sunshine, and you by my side;
'T is just such an evening to dream of in sleep;
'T is just such a joy to remember and weep;
Never before since you called me your own
Were you, I, and nature so proudly alone—
Cushlamachree, 't is blessèd to be
All the long summer eve talking to thee.

ELLEN MARY PATRICK DOWNING

July 21

I LOVED A love—a royal love—
In the golden long ago;
And she was fair as fair could be,
The foam upon the broken sea,
The sheen of sun, or moon, or star,
The sparkle from the diamond spar,
Not half so rare and radiant are
As my own love—my royal love—
In the golden long ago.

EDMUND LEAMY

June 29

BETTER TODAY than tomorrow morning.

IRISH PROVERB

July 20

"**H**OW STRANGE one never tires of the lark!" said the gentlest of my gentle cousins, Annie.

MATTHEW RUSSELL

June 30

Lovely Mary Donnelly

OH, LOVELY Mary Donnelly, it's you I love the best!
If fifty girls were round you I'd hardly see the rest.
Be what it may the time of day, the place be where
   it will,
Sweet looks of Mary Donnelly, they bloom before
   me still.

WILLIAM ALLINGHAM

July 19

FROM WHAT dripping cell, through what fairy glen,
Where 'mid old rocks and ruins the fox makes his den,
Over what lonesome mountain,
Acuishle mo chroidhe!
Where gauger never has trod,
Sweet as the flowery sod,
Wild as the breath
Of the breeze on the heath,
And sparking all o'er like the moon-lighted fountain,
Are you come to me—
Sorrowful me?

JOSEPH SHERIDAN LE FANU

July 2

THAT WAS *excellently observed*, say I, when I read a passage in an author where his opinion agrees with mine. When we differ, there I pronounce him to be *mistaken*.

JONATHAN SWIFT

July 17

SIMPLE DAYS bring simple joys...

EMILY LAWLESS

July 3

Drinking Song

Here's to the maiden of bashful fifteen,
Here's to the widow of fifty;
Here's to the flaunting extravagant quean,
And here's to the housewife that's thrifty:
Chorus:
Let the toast pass,
Drink to the lass,
I'll warrant she'll prove an excuse for the glass.

RICHARD BRINSLEY SHERIDAN

July 16

A Guinness Legacy

THE GUINNESS family, the noted Irish brewers, regularly contributed to the renovation of St. Patrick's Cathedral over the years. It is therefore interesting to note that a monument to Sir Benjamin Guinness's daughter stands under a stained glass window bearing the words, "I was thirsty and ye gave me drink."

July 4

THIS HEART
thy pillow.

SAMUEL LOVER

July 15

PHYSICALLY, MEN have the indisputable superiority in strength, and women in beauty.

WILLIAM E. H. LECKY

July 5

Across the Sea

THERE'S JOY in the hopeful morning,
There's peace in the parting day,
There's sorrow with every lover
Whose true-love is far away...

WILLIAM ALLINGHAM

July 14

Hills as green as emeralds
Cover the countryside
Lakes as blue as sapphires—
Are Ireland's special pride
And rivers that shine like silver
Make Ireland look so fair—
But the friendliness of her people
Is the richest treasure there.

IRISH BLESSING

July 6

Our Irish blunders
are never blunders
of the heart.

MARIA EDGEWORTH

July 13

THE RAINBOW gleams of a world unknown.

THOMAS W. HAZEN ROLLESTON

July 7

I AM A wand'ring minstrel man,
And Love my only theme;
I've strayed beside the pleasant Bann,
And eke the Shannon's stream;
I've piped and played to wife and maid
By Barrow, Suir, and Nore
But never met a maiden yet
Like *Brihidin ban mo store.**

EDWARD WALSH
* BRIDGET, MY TREASURE

July 12

Kate of Arraglen

WHEN I first saw thee, Kate,
That summer ev'ning late,
Down at the orchard gate
Of Arraglen,
I felt I'd ne'er before
Seen one so fair, asthore,
I feared I'd never more
See thee again—
I stopped and gazed at thee,
My footfall luckily
Reached not thy ear,
though we
Stood there so near;
While from thy lips a strain,
Soft as the summer rain,
Sad as a lover's pain
Fell on my ear.

DENNY LANE

July 8

TAKE A blessing from my heart to the
  land of my birth,
And the fair hills of Eiré O!

DONOGH MAC CON-MARA

July 11

THE EYE of a friend is a good looking glass.

IRISH PROVERB

July 9

&

Let schoolmasters puzzle their brain,
With grammar, and nonsense, and
   learning;
Good liquor, I stoutly maintain,
Gives genius a better discerning.

Oliver Goldsmith

July 10

AND THOUGH many an isle be fair,
Fairer still is Inisfallen...

WILLIAM LARMINIE